Thirtysomething

A patchwork pattern . . .

Acknowledgments

Thanks once again to all my family, friends, students and fellow quilting professionals for believing in me. Lisa Bong, Mark Bong, Shirley Scharnoski, Sarah Surroz, Sue Bong, Pat Titus, Nancy Linz, Peggy Taggart, Margot Schumacher, Chris Lynn Kirsch, Kelly Kroon, Elinor Czarnecki, Mary Cordes, Sheila Marie, Rosemary Schmidt, Trudie Hughes, Paula Lucas and all the rest, I couldn't have done it without you. All help in the way of moral support, pattern testing, self-publishing lessons, designing and quiltmaking, etc. is sincerely appreciated.

About The Author

Gayle Bong has been designing and making quilts since 1981. She began teaching quilting in 1988. Soon after, her first book, *Infinite Stars,* was published. The 60° angle continued to intrigue her with its possibilities for design and her second book, *Trouble Free Triangles,* was the result. It's not likely her love affair with rotary cutting, designing patchwork quilts, and teaching will end any time soon. Gayle lives with her husband, Mark, and daughter, Lisa in rural Elkhorn, Wisconsin. In her spare time she enjoys gardening and hiking in the fields and wooded hills around her home.

Thirtysomething
© Copyright 1997
By Gayle Bong
Photography by Bruce Thompson Studios

Published in the United States by
PL publications, Lake Geneva, Wisconsin

ISBN: 0-9654580-1-6 $19.00

 **Gaylee Quilting**
N 6628 Bowers Road
Elkhorn, WI 53121
(414) 723-7873

Table Of Contents

Introduction

The concept for Thirtysomething was conceived while I was working on my first book, Infinite Stars. I had used 30° and 60° angles in the stars and I was looking for a corner treatment for the borders. I reasoned that if a corner of a square is a 90° angle, then three 30° angles could join to form the corner. Not one to draft and use templates, I cut oversized 60° triangles in half, sewed three together and squared up the unit. Thirtysomething materialized right before my eyes.

  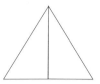

After I made those first four corner units, I placed them together on the table and saw a simple four-pointed star. I didn't think much more about them until I noticed a similar unit in a number of traditional blocks. I decided to explore the design possibilities I knew an asymmetrical unit like this possessed. Manipulating the unit in groups to form "traditional blocks" was fun. As my collection of new designs grew, I eagerly shared the concept with my classes. Their excitement was very encouraging.

The Thirtysomething unit is easily confused with the traditional unit based on a grid. The traditional unit requires two templates with different angles and trying to align them correctly for sewing can be difficult. A Thirtysomething unit is based on the division of a 90° corner. Changing the angle of all three pieces to 30°, makes both cutting and sewing easier. By cutting rectangles in half diagonally for all three pieces, I've eliminated the need for templates. With all three angles the same, there is no need to guess how to align the points for sewing, simply match the points and sew.

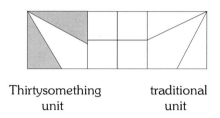

Thirtysomething   traditional
unit   unit

All the quilts in this book use rotary cutting techniques; just an explanation of the Thirtysomething concept is presented. It is assumed you already have a basic understanding of quiltmaking and rotary cutting. If you need a refresher on basic quiltmaking techniques, see your local quilt shop for one of the numerous books available on the subject.

In addition to the thirteen quilts featured in the pattern section, the gallery shows creative options for several of the patterns. Tips are included for making these. Other quilts in the gallery show the versatility of the concept, and are included to inspire you to begin your own Thirtysomething quilt.

I am sure you'll agree, Thirtysomething provides an easy and accurate way to cut and piece exciting new designs. Have fun as you use the new techniques I've presented to make your new favorite quilt!

– Gayle Bong

Tools

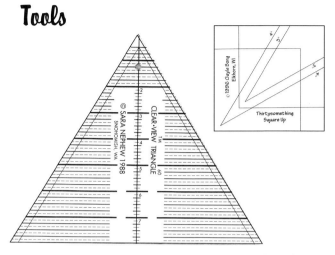

A basic rotary cutting set is needed for cutting: a 24" straight edge ruler for cutting strips, a rotary cutter and mat. In addition, the Thirtysomething Square Up is a useful cutting guide that I designed especially for this technique. The tool will true units to 3½" or 4½", though any size is possible with the technique. The Thirtysomething Square Up is less confusing to use and more accurate than just using a square ruler, however, a square ruler is adaptable.

Directions for cutting some of the pieces are shown using an equilateral triangle ruler. The 6" Clearview Triangle™ by Sara Nephew is suggested. It is available through mail order or your local quilt shop. Beware that other brands of equilateral triangle rulers are marked differently. A basic strip cutting ruler marked with a 60° angle may be used. A little playing and you should be able to figure out how to cut equilateral triangles. Directions and diagrams aren't given for using these tools, but I have included hints that should help.

Before We Begin

All pieces are rotary cut from strips cut across the width of fabric 42" wide. Measurements for sashing, setting triangles, half-square and quarter-square triangles include the quilters ¼" seam allowance.

Pieces for Thirtysomething units, onlies and the Fancy X block are not cut the exact size needed. A bit extra has been added to trim off and to allow for *slight* variations in seam width. Still, care should be taken in both cutting and piecing to maintain the correct angles.

Half-square Triangles

A few of the designs use these triangles. They are cut from squares. Cut the fabric into strips the width required for the quilt plan. Cut squares. (3⅞" to finish 3" or 4⅞" to finish 4".) For half-square triangles, cut the squares in half diagonally from corner to corner. This places the bias on the long edge of the triangle.

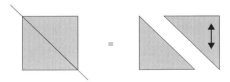

Quarter-square Triangles

Cut squares the size indicated in the pattern. (4¼" to finish 3" or 5¼" to finish 4".) Cut the squares in fourths diagonally. Cut both diagonals before moving the fabric. This places the bias on the short edge of the triangle.

Thirtysomething

Thirtysomething Units

The pieces in Thirtysomething units are half-triangles (equilateral triangles cut in half), but it is easier to just cut rectangles diagonally. The rectangles are not in the usual 1 to 2 ratio because they would not yield the 30° angles which are required. The three half-triangles in the unit are labeled A, B, and C consistently throughout the book. The center (C) half-triangle is cut from a larger rectangle and then trimmed square after it is sewn.

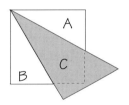

Rectangles are cut from strips either the rectangles length or width. The patterns usually use the rectangles length as the strip width. Notice that A triangles are the mirror image of B triangles. They may be cut from rectangles in one of two ways. The patterns indicate how to cut them and the direction of the diagonal.

Rectangle Size Needed	
3" finished units	
A & B triangles	2½" x 4¼"
C triangles	3⅜" x 5¾"
4" finished units	
A & B triangles	3⅛" x 5⅜"
C triangles	4" x 6⅞"

Method 1. Cut strips selvage to selvage the width indicated in the pattern. With strips folded in half once, *wrong sides together*, cut rectangles the measurement indicated in the pattern. Cut rectangles diagonally for A, B and C triangles. The triangles will be back to back. For less confusion when you sew, take the time to stack the A triangles and B triangles in separate piles.

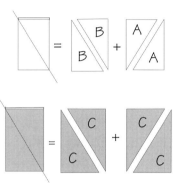

Method 2. To cut all A triangles, cut strips selvage to selvage the width indicated in the pattern. Open fabric and layer strips *right side up.* Cut rectangles the measurement indicated in the pattern or the chart below. Place rectangles vertically on the mat and cut them diagonally from lower left to upper right.

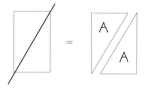

To cut all B triangles, cut strips selvage to selvage the width indicated in the pattern. Open fabric and layer strips *right side up.* Cut rectangles the measurement indicated in the pattern or the chart below. Place rectangles vertically on the mat and cut them diagonally from lower right to upper left.

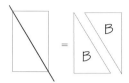

Cut rectangles for C triangles from strips, too. C triangles for Thirtysomething units may be cut from a folded strip. But if the C triangles are for the Fancy X block, open fabric and layer strips right side up, then cut rectangles. Cut the rectangles diagonally from lower right to upper left, and trim the tips for the C triangles used in the Fancy X block. See page 11. Do not trim for Thirtysomething units.

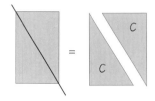

This chart will help you calculate yardage needed for your Thirtysomething design.

Triangles per 40" Strip

	Strip Width	Rectangle Length	Quantity
3" units			
A or B	$2\frac{1}{2}$"	$4\frac{1}{4}$"	18
	$4\frac{1}{4}$"	$2\frac{1}{2}$"	32
C	$3\frac{3}{8}$"	$5\frac{3}{4}$"	12
	$5\frac{3}{4}$"	$3\frac{3}{8}$"	22
4" units			
A or B	$3\frac{1}{8}$"	$5\frac{3}{8}$"	14
	$5\frac{3}{8}$"	$3\frac{1}{8}$"	24
C	4"	$6\frac{7}{8}$"	10
	$6\frac{7}{8}$"	4"	20

Sewing
Thirtysomething Units

Sew the A triangle to the C triangle first, matching angles precisely. Start stitching at the broad edge of the C triangle rather than at the point. The smaller A triangle will be underneath. Don't be concerned that you will be sewing through a single layer of fabric (patch C) for an inch or so.

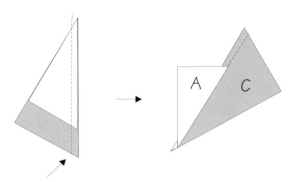

Flip over and begin sewing from this end.

Press the seam allowance toward the A triangle. Hold the point straight while pressing. Press carefully to avoid tucks, particularly at the point. Do not trim the point until after the B triangle is sewn on. The point is needed to align the B triangle.

Add a B triangle, matching the three narrow points precisely. Start stitching at the broad end of the C triangle. The small B triangle will now be on top. Press the seam toward the B triangle. Hold the point straight while pressing. Use care not to stretch when pressing.

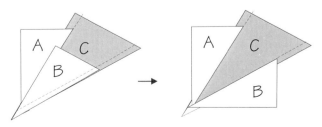

Thirtysomething

Squaring Up

The Thirtysomething Square Up tool was designed to trim Thirtysomething units that finish either 3" or 4" including seam allowances. It is the exact size of the 4" unit (4½" with seam allowances). Simply align the angled lines marked 4" with the seam lines of the Thirtysomething unit and trim everything extending beyond the edges.

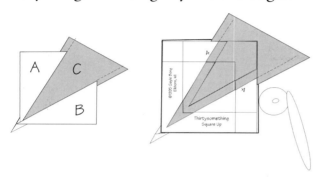

For the 3" units (3½" with seam allowances), align the inner set of angled lines marked 3" with the seams of the unit. Trim the C triangle and any excess fabric adjacent to it.

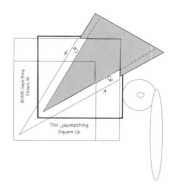

Use scissors to trim the pointy seam allowance, or if necessary, rotate both the Thirtysomething unit and the Square Up and align the angled lines marked 4" with the seams of the 3" unit. Trim the points and any excess fabric.

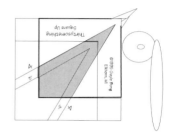

To use an ordinary square quilter's ruler position the unit as shown. Place the ruler so the edges of the A and B triangles are aligned with either the 3½" or 4½" lines of the ruler. The 1⅜" mark on the ruler should meet the seamlines at the edges of the 3" unit. The 1¹³⁄₁₆" mark on the ruler should meet the seamlines at the edges of the 4" unit. Trim the C triangle and any excess fabric adjacent to it, then trim the points.

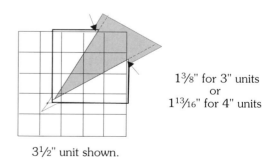

1⅜" for 3" units
or
1¹³⁄₁₆" for 4" units

3½" unit shown.

Rotary Cutting

Onlies

Some designs will require units with only 1 A or 1 B and no C's. The A or B triangle is cut the same as when both are used in the Thirtysomething unit. Piece D, and E, its reverse, are cut from squares. The patterns in the book using onlies require angles to be trimmed off pairs of squares placed wrong sides together (a strip folded once). Cut squares $3\frac{1}{2}$" x $3\frac{1}{2}$" for the 3" units and $4\frac{1}{2}$" x $4\frac{1}{2}$" for 4" units.

Place the center line of the Clearview Triangle on an edge of the square as shown below. Measure $\frac{3}{8}$" less than the height of the square and cut off a 30-60-90° triangle as shown.

Squares wrong sides together.

Sew on an A or B triangle making it square again. To align the pieces for sewing, offset the half-triangle so that its 60° corner creates a $\frac{1}{4}$" wide triangle extending past piece D or E. Start sewing at this wide end of the half-triangle. Press the seam allowance in opposite directions in the two units.

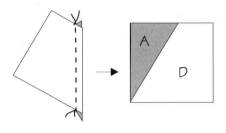

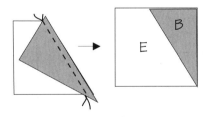

Trim the 3" onlies to $3\frac{1}{2}$" square. Trim the 4" onlies to $4\frac{1}{2}$" square. Trim the excess from the A or B patch.

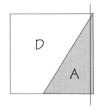

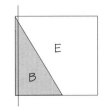

Fancy X

Grouping four Thirtysomething units with the narrow points of the C triangle pointing in resembles a simplified kaleidoscope block. I call it the Fancy X block. Sewing this block can be somewhat difficult because twelve seams come together in the center. This is unnecessary if neighboring A's and B's are the same fabric. It is better to eliminate the seam and cut equilateral triangles to use in place of the two half-triangles. The Fancy X block finishes 6" where 3" units would have been used and 8" where 4" units would have been used.

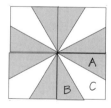 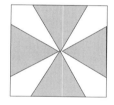

Equilateral Triangles for Fancy X

Cut strips the width indicated in the pattern, either 4" wide for 6" blocks or 5" wide for 8" blocks. Place the triangle ruler on the strip with the corresponding ruled line even with the lower edge of the strip. The point of the ruler should meet the upper edge of the strip, yet not extend beyond it. Cut on each side of the triangle ruler.

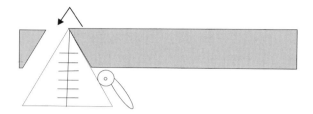

For successive cuts, slide the triangle ruler over only until the side of the ruler comes to the point of the next triangle (on the lower edge of the fabric). Cut on both sides of the triangle ruler again and continue across the strip. There is no need to flip the ruler and you may work from right to left or left to right. Stack equilateral triangles so the grain line is on the same edge.

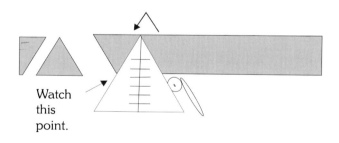

Watch this point.

To use another brand ruler marked with the 60° angle, follow these tips. Use the same strip width indicated in the patterns to cut equilateral triangles. Disregard the numbers and other markings on the ruler, instead focus on cutting the proper angle. Be sure each successive cut comes to the point of the wide angle. A sharp point is needed on all three corners of the triangle, not a blunted tip. Cut enough just to make a sample block to check for accuracy before continuing.

A patchwork pattern . . . with a kite-shaped patch

Trimming the C Triangles

Mark the seam line at the points on the wrong side of the fabric or trim the pointy seam allowance of the C triangle to match the seam allowance of the equilateral triangle. This would eliminate the need to guess how much to offset the C patch before sewing. Place a piece of $\frac{1}{4}$" wide masking tape along the right side of the center line of the ruler (when viewed from the front). Place the tape on the back of the Clearview Triangle.

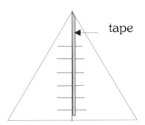

tape

Following the diagram below, *carefully* position the Clearview Triangle on the C triangles placed right side up so the right hand edge of the tape is at the right hand edge of the C triangle and the edge of the Clearview Triangle is on the opposite edge of the C triangle. Trim the tip of the C triangle extending beyond the tip of the ruler. Trimming is not suggested before sewing Thirtysomething units.

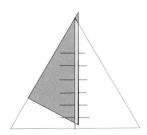

Sewing the Fancy X

Sew a C triangle to an equilateral triangle, positioning the grainline of the equilateral triangle toward the outside edge of the block. Press seam allowance toward the equilateral triangle.

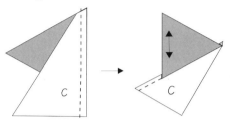

C   C

Sew two sets together, matching center points. Do not sew into the seam allowance at the center of the block.

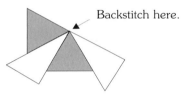

Backstitch here.

Join the two half-blocks. Press the seam allowances in a circular direction.

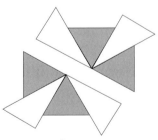

Square up each corner using the Thirtysomething Square Up as directed for individual units. Trim the blocks to $6\frac{1}{2}$" square or $8\frac{1}{2}$" square.

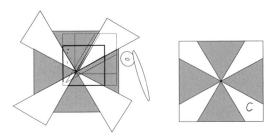

C

A patchwork pattern . . . or a pieced unit

Points to Remember

- Match raw edges carefully when layering strips right side up.
- Hold ruler firmly and make diagonal cuts before moving the rectangle to minimize fabric shifting.
- Be sure to cut all rectangles diagonally while placed vertically on the mat.

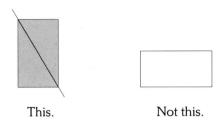

This.   Not this.

- How do you know if the triangle is an A or a B? The first line in the letter A is at an angle like the first line of the A patch. The first line in the letter B is vertical like the first line of the B patch when fabric is placed right side up.

- To match points, simply line up both raw edges at the point of the two patches.

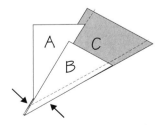

- Cut C triangles for the Fancy X block with fabric layered right side up.
- Always sew the *long* bias edge of the A and B triangles to the C triangle. This will place the straight of grain at the edges of the unit.

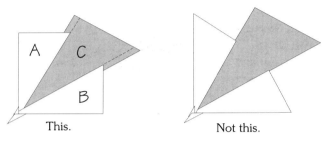

This.   Not this.

- The C triangle may point in two directions. Ignore this as you sew.

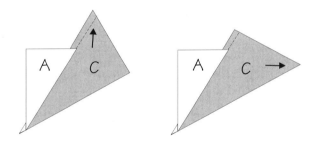

- If you stretch the bias when pressing, the angle of the C triangle will be greater than the angled lines of the Thirtysomething Square Up. You may think you cut or sewed something wrong. By holding the corner where the three triangles meet and the opposite end of the C triangle, gently stretch the triangle back into shape.

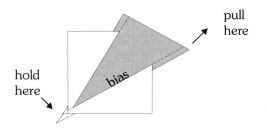

pull here

hold here

bias

Some Vital Basics

Quilt Assembly & Pressing

I begin to use pins once all the units for a quilt are made and I start to stitch them together. Sewing through the many layers at seam intersections is the cause of many misaligned points. I use a single pin parallel to the seam, leaving it in as long as possible. My sewing machine is sensitive to pins under her feet and distorts the seam the second a pin gets underfoot. I position the pin so that it slides up between her toes. As I approach the intersection, I very gradually withdraw the pin. (And all the while watching my seam allowance!) This is what works for me. Experiment with different ways to pin to avoid shifting. Every machine seems to handle fabric differently.

As the quilt progresses, the Thirty-something units will dictate the direction to press the seams. Press away from the points if at all possible. Often twisted seams will result. This is OK. To minimize a seam appearing to be twisted, press it to one side first. A little steam flattens it all the more.

Seam Allowances

Next to finding time to sew, sewing an accurate seam allowance is probably the biggest piecing challenge you will face. Pass this simple test for crisp points and perfectly matched seam intersections.

Cut three pieces of fabric, each $1\frac{1}{2}$" x 5". Sew them together with a $\frac{1}{4}$" wide seam allowance. Press and measure the width of the three strip unit. It should now equal exactly $3\frac{1}{2}$", with the center strip measuring 1". When the correct seam allowance is

taken, you may notice that it is actually a scant $\frac{1}{4}$" wide. This is necessary to obtain the correct finished dimensions of any rotary cut project. If it does not, repeat the test, adjusting the seam allowance by taking a slightly wider or narrower seam until you find the correct width.

Some machines do this simply by changing presser feet or moving the needle. When you find the proper place to position your fabric, mark the throat plate with several layers of masking tape. Feeding the fabric against the edge of the layered tape will help relieve eye strain and help you sew more quickly. Repeat the test with the tape in place to be certain it is positioned accurately.

each $1\frac{1}{2}$ cut

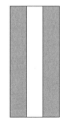

$3\frac{1}{2}$" sewn

Design Inspiration

Because of its' diagonal nature, the Thirtysomething unit is amazingly versatile. A wide variety of designs can be achieved by using the unit exclusively in the quilt, combining it with other common units to make patchwork blocks and used in place of other units in traditional patchwork blocks. Combining these options with the twenty or more different settings for blocks and altering the placement of lights, mediums and darks leads to more designs.

I particularly enjoy changing a quilt plan to create a new design and have left the quilt diagram with each pattern blank for you to experiment with color. Copy those pages and recolor with the color of your choice, change positions of light, medium and dark, or eliminate or change some of the units used. Many variations are possible. Included here are just a few more block ideas from mine and my daughter's sketchbook.

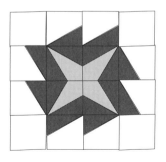

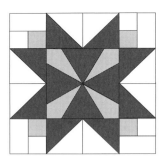

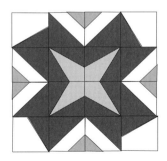

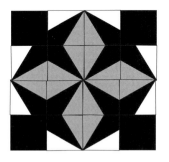

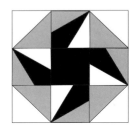 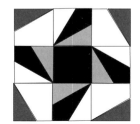

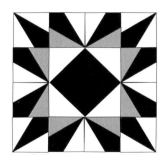

Using the Patterns

It is a good idea to read the preceding pages before beginning your quilt. This is a new technique and I have tried to include little that you already know.

Prior to beginning, read all the directions for the particular quilt you are making. Consider practicing this new technique on scraps to test your understanding of the directions. After making a few practice pieces, you can chain piece when you begin your quilt.

Yardage requirements are based on fabric 40" wide after selvages are removed.

Ironing fabric with spray starch before beginning to cut will help control the bias. Spray and iron it twice with spray starch, and it will almost be like working with paper; and paper doesn't have a bias. Yeah!

All strips are cut selvage to selvage.

All measurements already include a ¼" seam allowance. It is advisable by many top quilting teachers to satisfy the seam test on page 13 before beginning. I hope you will take the time to do it.

Double the number of rectangles in the chart to determine the number of A, B and C triangles needed for the pattern.

Half-square triangle units are used in a few of the quilt plans. Fabric requirements are adequate to substitute the technique of your choice for cutting and piecing these.

Material requirements for borders are based on quilts with blunted corners rather than mitered corners. Border strips are cut crosswise, selvage to selvage and joined end to end where necessary for the required length. Be certain to measure through the center of the quilt and along the two parallel edges to find the average length and cut strips to this length.

Although the technique is adaptable to any size, I developed the technique using 3" and 4" finished units because they are most compatible with other patchwork blocks. The patterns are written for the 3" unit, with the exception of some size options but the 4" Thirtysomething unit can be substituted. The 3" is more appropriate for the wall or lap quilts shown, while the 4" unit is more compatible with full size bed quilts. **Keep in mind the sashing and other setting pieces in the quilt would need to be enlarged as well.** Changing the pattern from 3" to 4" enlarges it by 25 percent. Approximately 25 percent or one/fourth more fabric would be required.

Pattern Key

⊡ squares cut once diagonally

⊠ squares cut twice diagonally

▨ direction of diagonal cut for B & C triangles

▧ direction of diagonal cut for A triangles

◺ half-square triangles

△ quarter square triangles

Dress Rehearsal

This is a great warm-up project with only 20 units to make. To float the stars, use the same fabric for the sash as the background of the stars.

Color photo: page 25

Block size: 7½"
Quilt size: 32" x 32"
Materials:
  stars – ¼ yd.
  background – 1 yd.
  sashing – ⅜ yd.
  border – ½ yd.
  binding – ⅜ yd.
  backing – 1 yd.

Cutting

Read using the patterns on page 15 before beginning to cut.

*Open fabric right side up and cut 10 light rectangles 4¼" x 2½". Cut diagonally for 20 A triangles. ◹

**Open fabric right side up and cut 10 light rectangles 4¼" x 2½". Cut diagonally for 20 B triangles. ◺

***Cut rectangles 5¾" x 3⅜". Cut diagonally for 20 C triangles. ◿

FABRIC	STRIP WIDTH	NO. OF STRIPS	SUBCUTTING
background	4¼"	1	10 rectangles*
	4¼"	1	10 rectangles**
	3½"	1	20 rectangles 2" wide
	12"	1	1 ⊠ for 4 △ and 2 ◳ 7" x 7" for 4 ◺
stars	5¾"	1	10 rectangles*** and 5 squares, 2" x 2"
sashing	2½"	4	2 strips 26" long, 4 strips 12" long, and 6 strips 8" long
border	3½"	4	
binding	2½"	4	

A patchwork pattern . . . not a tv show

Piecing

1. Piece 20 Thirtysomething units as directed on page 7. Trim units to 3½" square.

Make 20

2. Piece 5 blocks following the block piecing diagram below.

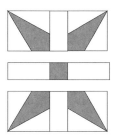 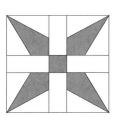

Make 5

3. Following the illustration, assemble the pieced blocks, sashing and side setting triangles in diagonal rows. Sew the rows together keeping the corners of blocks lined up with one another. Add the corners and adjacent sashing strip last.

4. Straighten the edges of the quilt top. Add borders, referring to directions on page 15 for measuring the correct length.

First Act

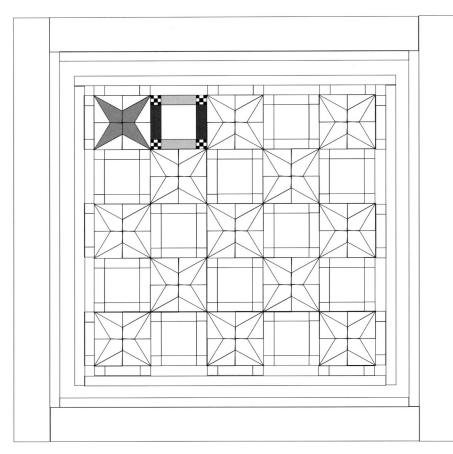

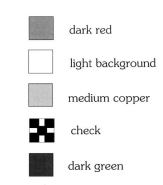

dark red

light background

medium copper

check

dark green

Block size: 6"

Quilt size: 46" x 46"

Materials:
 dark red – 1¾ yds.
 light background – 1¼ yds.
 medium copper – ½ yd.
 check – ¼ yd.
 dark green – ⅝ yd.
 backing – 2¾ yds.
 binding – ½ yd.

Who would have thought combining a simple four-pointed star with the uneven nine-patch would have made such a popular quilt. To add a little interest, make each star from a different fabric, or try two-tone stars.
Color photo: page 25

 *Cut red rectangles 5¾" x 3⅜". Cut diagonally for 52 C triangles.
 **Layer fabric right side up and cut light rectangles 4¼" x 2½". Cut diagonally for 52 A triangles.
 ***Layer fabric right side up and cut light rectangles 4¼" x 2½". Cut diagonally for 52 B triangles.

Cutting

Read using the patterns on page 15 before beginning to cut.

FABRIC	STRIP WIDTH	NO. OF STRIPS	SUBCUTTING
dark red	5¾"	3	26 rectangles*
	4"	5	border
	2½"	5	binding
light	4¼"	2	26 rectangles**
	4¼"	2	26 rectangles***
	4½"	2	
	1½"	2	8 rectangles 6½" long, and 4 squares
	1½"	4	border
med. copper	1½"	4	
	2"	4	border
check	1½"	3	
dark green	4½"	2	
	1½"	4	border

Piecing

1. Piece 52 dark red Thirtysomething units as directed on page 7. Trim to $3\frac{1}{2}$" square. Make 13 star blocks.

Make 52.   Make 13 stars.

2. Sew 2 sets from the $1\frac{1}{2}$" medium copper and $4\frac{1}{2}$" light strips. Press seam allowance toward the copper. Cut into 12 rectangles $4\frac{1}{2}$" wide.

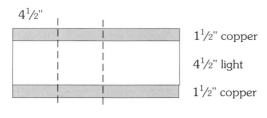

4½"

1½" copper
4½" light
1½" copper

Make 2 sets.

3. Cut a $1\frac{1}{2}$" strip of check in half and sew $1\frac{1}{2}$ sets from the $1\frac{1}{2}$" check and $4\frac{1}{2}$" dark green strips. Press seam allowance toward the green. Cut into 36 segments $1\frac{1}{2}$" wide.

1½"

1½" check
4½" green
1½" check

Make 1½ sets.

4. Sew the green rectangle units to the copper units to complete the nine-patch blocks.

5. Sew the blocks together, alternating them throughout the quilt as shown.

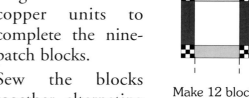

Make 12 blocks.

6. Piece 4 border strips, alternating 3 green units with light rectangles. Sew 2 border strips to opposite sides of the quilt. Sew the light squares to opposite ends of the 2 remaining border strips. Sew to the top and bottom of quilt.

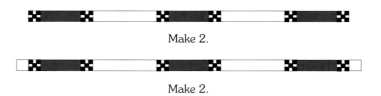

Make 2.

Make 2.

7. Add plain borders, referring to directions on page 15 for measuring the correct length.

Size Option

In the queen size variation, the large square is cut from a large scale medium print and all the bars are cut from one fabric. Convert to 4" units and piece 50 stars. Make 49 uneven nine-patch blocks 8" square. Add borders cut $6\frac{1}{2}$" wide for a quilt 87" x 103" before quilting. The queen size variation requires:

- $2\frac{1}{2}$ yds. or $\frac{1}{4}$ yd. each of 10 different reds
- $2\frac{3}{4}$ yds. light for star background
- $1\frac{1}{4}$ yds. medium print for big squares
- 2 yds. medium green for bars
- $\frac{3}{4}$ yd. dark green for small squares
- $1\frac{3}{4}$ yds. for binding
- $7\frac{1}{2}$ yds. for backing

A patchwork pattern . . . with design potential

Firedance

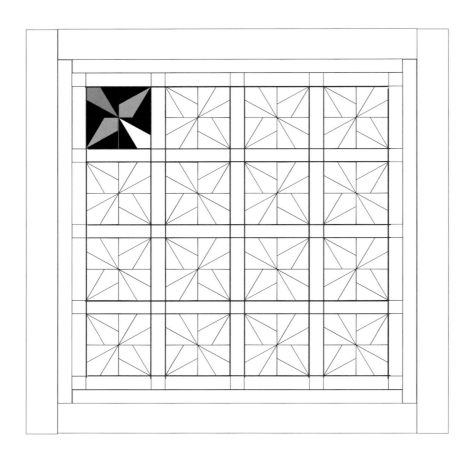

Repositioning the units in the simple four-pointed star with two units pointing in and two pointing out gives us another simple block. The sashing and corner squares contribute to the illusion of circles.

Color photo: page 27

Block size: 6"
Quilt size: 42" x 42"
Materials:
yellow – ¼ yd.
orange – ⅛ yd.
red – ⅛ yd.
blue – ¼ yd.
green – ½ yd.
black – 1¾ yds.
backing – 2¾ yds.

Cutting

Read using the patterns on page 15 before beginning to cut.

*Cut rectangles 5¾" x 3⅜". Cut diagonally for C triangles.

**Layer fabric right side up and cut black rectangles 4¼" x 2½". Cut diagonally for 64 A triangles.

***Layer fabric right side up and cut black rectangles 4¼" x 2½". Cut diagonally for 64 B triangles.

FABRIC	STRIP WIDTH	NO. OF STRIPS	SUBCUTTING
yellow	5¾"	1	10 rectangles*, and 5 squares 2" x 2"
orange	3⅜"	1	4 rectangles*, and 2 squares 2" x 2"
red	3⅜"	1	4 rectangles*, and 2 squares 2" x 2"
green	5¾"	1	6 rectangles*, and 8 squares 2" x 2"
	2"	4	inner border
blue	5¾"	1	8 rectangles*, and 8 squares 2" x 2"
black	4¼"	2	32 rectangles**
	4¼"	2	32 rectangles***
	6½"	2	40 rectangles 2" wide
	4¼"	4	border
	2½"	4	binding

A patchwork pattern . . . and a fun technique

Piecing

1. Use all the colored C triangles with the black A and black B triangles to piece 64 Thirtysomething units as directed on page 7. Trim units to $3\frac{1}{2}$" square.

Make 20 yellow.   Make 8 orange.

Make 8 red.   Make 12 green.   Make 16 blue.

2. Combine the Thirtysomething units into the blocks shown. Make 4 of each block.

Make 4 of each block.

3. Arrange the blocks with sashing and setting squares in the order shown in the quilt, rotating the blocks where necessary. Sew the blocks into rows, pressing seam allowances toward the sashing. Sew the rows together.

4. Add the green borders, then the black borders, referring to directions on page 15 for measuring the correct length.

Soaring High

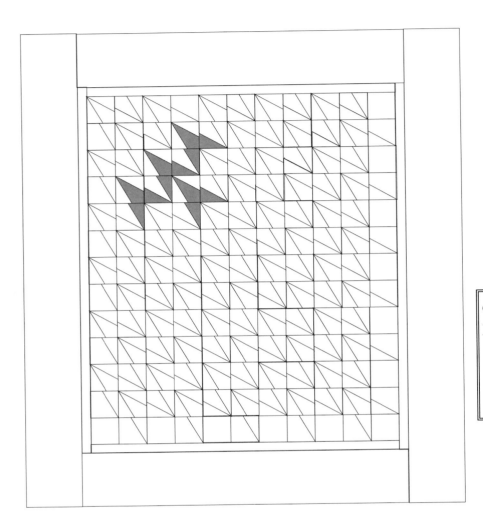

Two color quilts have always intrigued me with their graphic simplicity. Light, dark, light units and dark, light, dark units alternate throughout this quilt. Partial units around the edge of the pieced area are used to complete the dark soaring images. Several variations of this tessellation were just too good to resist. See "Dutch Caps" and "Always Look Up".

Color photo: page 23

Quilt size: 47" x 53"

Materials:
dark – 2½ yds.
light – 1⅜ yds.
accent – ¼ yd.
backing – 2¾ yds.

Cutting

Read using the patterns on page 15 before beginning to cut.

*Layer fabric right side up and cut rectangles 4¼" x 2½". Cut diagonally for 60 A triangles of each light and dark. ▨

**Layer fabric right side up and cut light rectangles 4¼" x 2½". Cut diagonally for 60 B triangles of each light and dark. ◹

***Cut rectangles 5¾" x 3⅜". Cut diagonally for C triangles. ◹

FABRIC	STRIP WIDTH	NO. OF STRIPS	SUBCUTTING
dark	4¼"	2	30 rectangles*
	4¼"	2	30 rectangles**
	5¾"	3	30 rectangles***
	6½"	5	borders
	2½"	5	binding
light	3½"	3	34 squares
	4¼"	2	30 rectangles*
	4¼"	2	30 rectangles**
	5¾"	2	25 rectangles***
accent	1½"	4	inner border

Piecing

1. Piece Thirtysomething units as directed on page 7. Trim to 3½" square. There will be 1 extra light C triangle.

Make 60   Make 49

2. Set aside 12 light squares. With 11 pairs of squares wrong sides together, trim the corner from squares to make onlies as directed on page 9. Piece 11 onlies and 11 onlies in reverse. Trim to 3½" square.

Make 11 of each.

3. Arrange the units following the diagram. Alternate the directions of the 2 different Thirtysomething units, and fill in the edges with plain squares and onlies as needed. Sew the units into rows, then sew the rows together. Press seam allowance away from points.

Point to remember: *The seams in the units do not meet when units are pointing in opposite directions.*

4. Add borders, referring to directions on page 15 for measuring the correct length.

Design Variation 1 – Dutch Caps

Pointing all units in the same direction results in this tessellating variation. Choose only 2 fabrics, or arrange color across the quilt from light to dark, or choose a scrappy assortment randomly placed. Sew all light, dark, light units first. Arrange color as desired. Then determine placement of fabrics in the dark, light, dark units. Onlies were also used at the edges and a narrow light border was added to only 2 sides. **Color photo: page 26**

> Unit size: 3"
> Quilt size: 43" x 48"
> Materials: 1¾ yds. light, and
>   ¼ yd. each of 9 different darks,
>   border, binding & backing to finish

Design Variation 2 – Always Look Up

In this variation of "Soaring High" multiple borders of bright scrappy squares surround the rainbow colored tesselation. Convert to 4" units and piece 108 units with black A and B triangles and colored C triangles (black, red, black, etc.) and piece 108 units with black C triangles and A and B triangles of the same color in each unit (red, black, red, etc.). Omit the onlies around the edge and border as desired.

Color photo: page 27

> Unit size: 4"
> Quilt size: 68" x 92"
> Materials: green – ½ yd.
>   yellow – ¾ yd.
>   orange – ¾ yd.
>   red – ¾ yd.
>   blue violet – ¾ yd.
>   aqua – ½ yd.
>   black – 5⅝ yds.
>   backing – 5½ yds.

Kissing Cousins

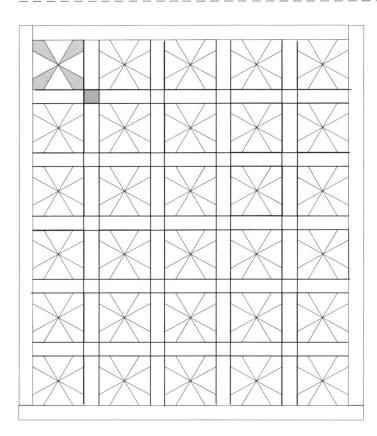

The inspiration for this quilt came from a collection of poorly cut antique diamond patches and the resemblance to an old quilt design I'd always intended to make. The diamonds were recut into the needed C triangles. And I was able to check off another quilt on my "gotta do" list.

Color photo: page 00

> **Block size:** 6"
> **Quilt size:** 41" x 49"
> **Materials:**
>   muslin – 1¾ yds.
>   scraps – 1¼ yds.
>   backing – 1½ yds.
>   binding – ½ yd.

*Cut rectangles 5¾" x 6¾". Cut 2 rectangles from each, 5¾" x 3⅜". Cut diagonally, right side up, for 4 C triangles of each fabric. Trim the tip of each C triangle as directed on page 11.

Cutting

Read using the patterns on page 15 before beginning to cut.

FABRIC	STRIP WIDTH	NO. OF STRIPS	SUBCUTTING
muslin	6½"	2	49 rectangles 2" wide
	4"	7	120 equilateral triangles
	2"	5	borders
binding	2½"	5	
scraps			30 different rectangles* and 20 squares 2" x 2"

Piecing

1. Piece 30 Fancy X blocks as directed on page 11. Trim to 6½" square.

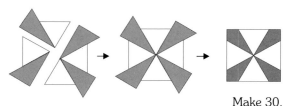

Make 30.

2. Alternating the blocks, sashing strips and 2" corner squares arrange the blocks in a pleasing order. Sew the blocks into rows. Sew the rows together. Press seam allowance toward sashing.

3. Add borders, referring to directions on page 15 for measuring the correct length.

Dress Rehearsal
by Gayle Bong,
Elkhorn, Wisconsin,
31" x 31".

These delightful
little stars can be
addicting. Watch
out! This could be
one of those quilts
that "grows".

Directions begin on
page 16.

First Act
by Gayle Bong,
Elkhorn, Wisconsin,
46" x 46".

This simple design
looks great in any
color scheme.
Altering placement
of lights and darks
works well, too.

Directions begin on
page 18.

A patchwork pattern . . . not a dress size

Soaring High
by Gayle Bong,
Elkhorn, Wisconsin,
47" x 53".

Choosing fabrics for this quilt is a snap. The accent color should be opposite the color wheel from the main fabric.

Directions begin on page 22.

Dutch Caps
by Gayle Bong,
Elkhorn, Wisconsin,
43" x 48".

The random placement of color with the light background is pleasing but if you're looking for a challenge, try a variety of light colored "caps" too.

See page 23.

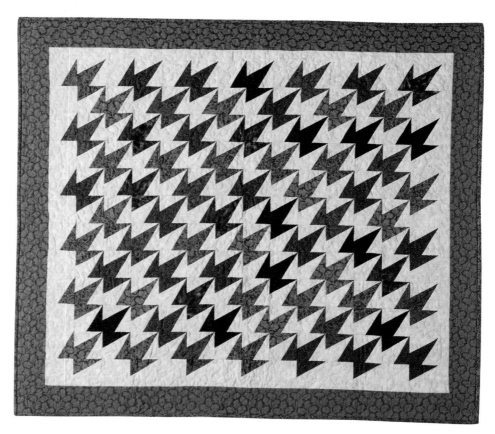

A patchwork pattern . . . that's easily made

Always Look Up
by Mary Cordes,
Cottage Grove, Wisconsin,
65" x 86".

Bold colors create a lively "Soaring High" variation.

See page 23.

Fire Dance
by Nancy Linz,
Mukwonago, Wisconsin,
38" x 38".

It's midnight, the fire is lit and the dance begins. Let's party!

Directions begin on page 20.

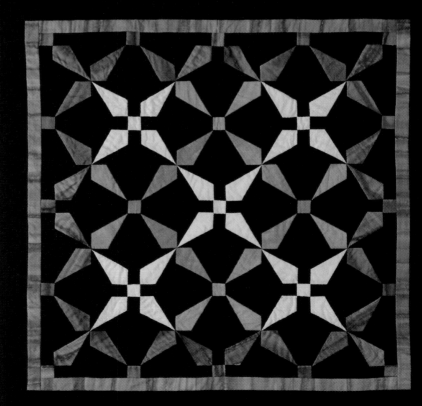

A patchwork pattern . . . with design potential

Rippling Water
by Gayle Bong,
Elkhorn, Wisconsin,
48" x 48".

Choose four shades
of blue to add to the
rippling effect or
simplify fabric selection
and choose one or
two colors.

Directions begin on
page 44.

Electrifying
Thirtysomething by
Rosemary Schmidt,
Madison, Wisconsin,
43" x 43".

Great bolts of
electricity are lighting
the midnight sky of
my mind, ever so
peacefully.

Directions begin on
page 40.

A patchwork pattern . . . with design potential

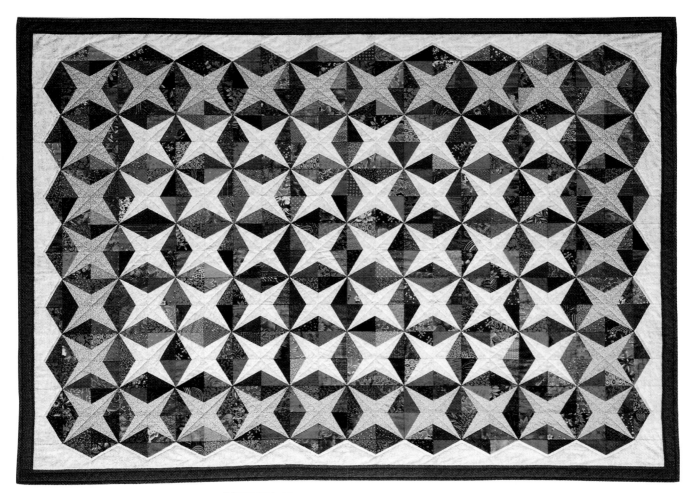

Sweet Pepper
by Gayle Bong,
Elkhorn, Wisconsin,
51" x 69".

The bright scraps make an
energetic quilt, just like
the cat it was named after.

Directions begin on
page 48.

Wish on a Rainbow
by Gayle Bong,
Elkhorn, Wisconsin,
54" x 54".

Each block is two color
wheels in one, with
complimentary colors
opposite each other.

Directions begin on
page 46.

A patchwork pattern . . . and a fun technique

Light in the Attic
by Margot Schumacher,
East Troy, Wisconsin,
62" x 62".

The changing scale gives depth to this design while the pieced border adds to the movement created by the color placement.

Opposites Attract
by Gayle Bong,
Elkhorn,
Wisconsin,
81" x 81".

The calico and soft colors give this design a traditional look.

Directions begin on page 53.

A patchwork pattern . . . with a kite-shaped patch

Kissing Cousins
by Gayle Bong,
Elkhorn,
Wisconsin,
38" x 45".

A collection of 1930's reproduction prints would look great in your copy of Kissing Cousins.

Directions begin on page 24.

Second Cousins
by Gayle Bong,
Elkhorn,
Wisconsin,
72" x 72".

Surprisingly, this quilt consists of nothing more than the Fancy X block.

Directions begin on page 50.

A patchwork pattern . . . or a pieced unit

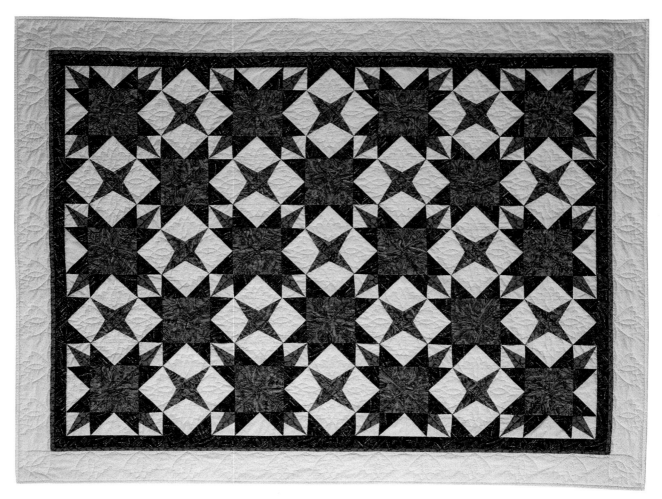

Star and Starlet
by Gayle Bong,
Elkhorn, Wisconsin,
60" x 78".

Here's evidence a new setting for a new star can result in a traditional quilt.

Directions begin on page 37.

Deep Sea
by Sue Bong,
Elkhorn, Wisconsin,
65" x 65".

These fish couldn't be easier with a pair of onlies and two half-square triangle units for each fish. Button eyes bring the fish to life.

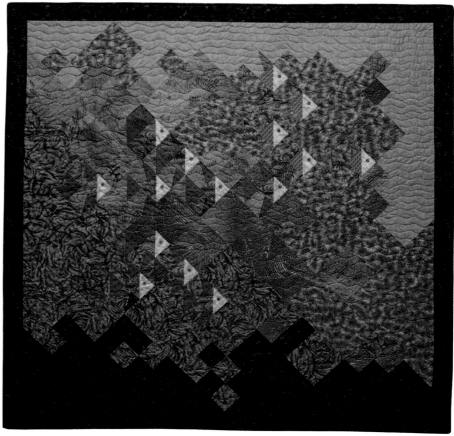

Toe Shoes and Tutus
by Gayle Bong, Elkhorn, Wisconsin, 88" x 88".

Ballerinas from above, performing in pink - I think I'll go to the ballet.

Directions begin on page 56.

Flight by Sheila Marie,
Woodridge, Illinois, 36" x 36".

Sheila's interpretation of Dutch Caps in
the M. C. Escher style is an excellent
example of how dramatically a design can
change when the values change.

Field of Black Eyed Susans
by Peggy Taggart,
Janesville, Wisconsin,
26" x 34".

The unique setting of the Fancy X
block is the foundation of this quilt,
embellished with buttons and
applique.

Celestial Pinwheels by Kelly Kroon,
Reedsburg, Wisconsin, 32" x 32".

Let these playful pinwheels take you back
to your childhood.

For random placement of color, construct
this quilt one pinwheel at a time.

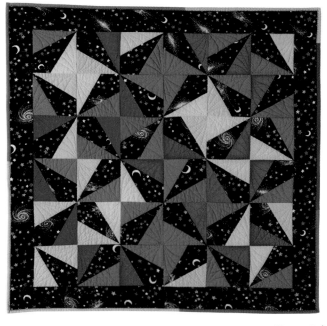

Whirlwind of Blues
by Lisa Bong,
Elkhorn, Wisconsin,
48" x 48".

The illusion of layers in
Lisa's quilt results from
the appropriate choice of
colors and values of the
fabrics in the design.
The border fabric adds
to the illusion of depth.

30° and Breezy?
by Chris Lynn Kirsch,
Oconomowoc,
Wisconsin, 66" x 66".

Chris successfully
created the illusion of
circles in her design.
The quilting is playing
with the triangles which
gives rise to the name.

A patchwork pattern . . . that's easily made

Oak Embers
by Gayle Bong,
Elkhorn, Wisconsin,
36" x 36".

Any color combination will work in this design. Let the wonderful fabrics available today inspire you.

See page 59.

Red Punch
by Gayle Bong,
Elkhorn, Wisconsin,
57" x 71".

The high contrast of the red and cream offers a crisp look, unmuddied by the warm brown.

See page 55.

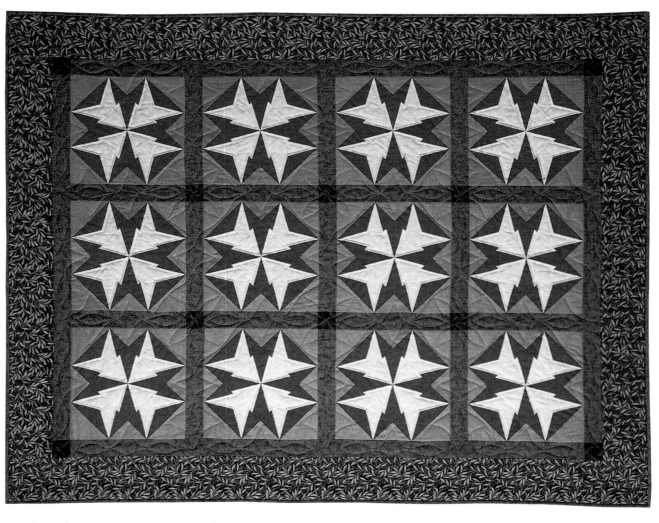

A patchwork pattern . . . not a tv show

Star and Starlet

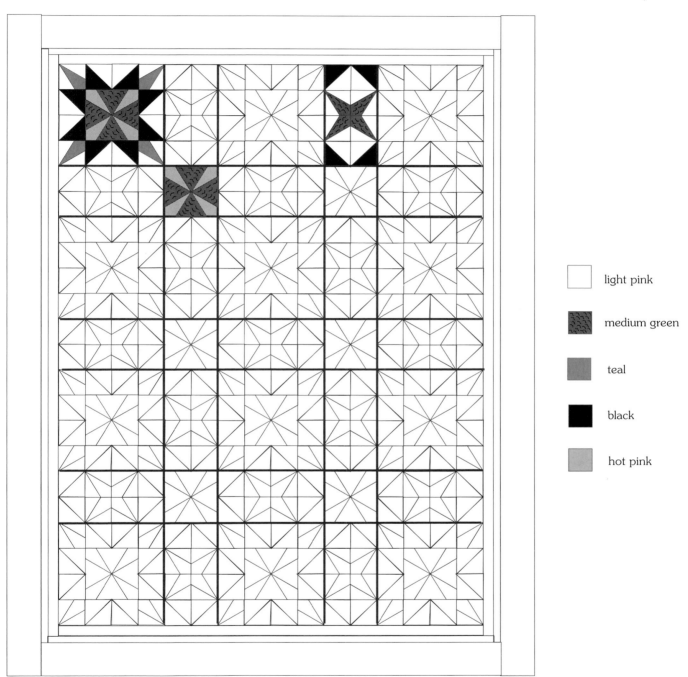

light pink

medium green

teal

black

hot pink

The Fancy X, Thirtysomething units and half-square triangle units are on parade here. The large star blocks appear to share corners thanks to a wide pieced sashing. The "shared corner" could be a simple 3½" square if you're in a hurry, or for another variation, substitute a four-pointed star for the Fancy X block.

Color photo: page 32

Block size: 12"

Quilt size: 60" x 80"

Materials:
 light pink – 3⅜ yds.
 black – 1½ yds.
 medium green – 1¼ yds.
 hot pink – ⅝ yd.
 medium teal – ¾ yd.
 backing – 3⅝ yds.
 binding – ¾ yd.

Cutting

Read using the patterns on page 15 before beginning to cut.

FABRIC	STRIP WIDTH	NO. OF STRIPS	SUBCUTTING
light pink	3⅞"	8	82◩ for 164 △
	4¼"	4	58 rectangles*
	4¼"	4	58 rectangles**
	4½"	7	outer border
medium green	4"	5	72 equilateral triangles
	5¾"	3	34 rectangles***
black	3⅞"	8	82◩ for 164 △
	2"	7	first border
hot pink	5¾"	3	36 rectangles***
medium teal	5¾"	2	24 rectangles***
	1"	7	second border
binding	2½"	7	

*Layer light pink fabric right side up and cut rectangles 4¼" x 2½". Cut diagonally for 116 A triangles. ◺

**Layer light pink fabric right side up and cut rectangles 4¼" x 2½". Cut diagonally for 116 B triangles. ◹

***Open strips and layer fabric right side up. Cut rectangles 5¾" x 3⅜". Cut diagonally for C triangles. Trim the tips off hot pink triangles as directed on page 11. ◱

A patchwork pattern . . . not a tv show

Piecing

1. Piece Thirtysomething units as directed on page 7. Trim to $3\frac{1}{2}$" square. Piece the light pink and green Thirtysomething units into 17 stars.

Make 48. Make 68.

Make 17.

2. Using green equilateral triangles and hot pink C triangles, piece 18 Fancy X blocks as directed on page 11. Trim to $6\frac{1}{2}$" square.

Make 18.

3. Place light pink and black triangles right sides together. Sew on the long edge. Press seam allowances toward the black. Sew into pairs.

Make 164.   Make 82.

4. Sew the light pink edge of pairs of half-square triangle units to opposite sides of the green stars for 17 sashing units.

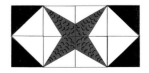

Make 17.

5. Piece 12 star blocks following the block piecing diagram. First join the units into 3 rows, then sew the rows together.

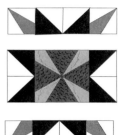 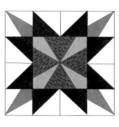

Make 12.

6. Sew the star blocks, Fancy X blocks and sashing units into rows as shown in the diagram. Sew the rows together.

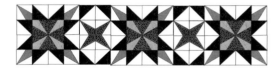

7. Add borders, referring to directions on page 15 for measuring the correct length.

Electrifying Thirtysomething

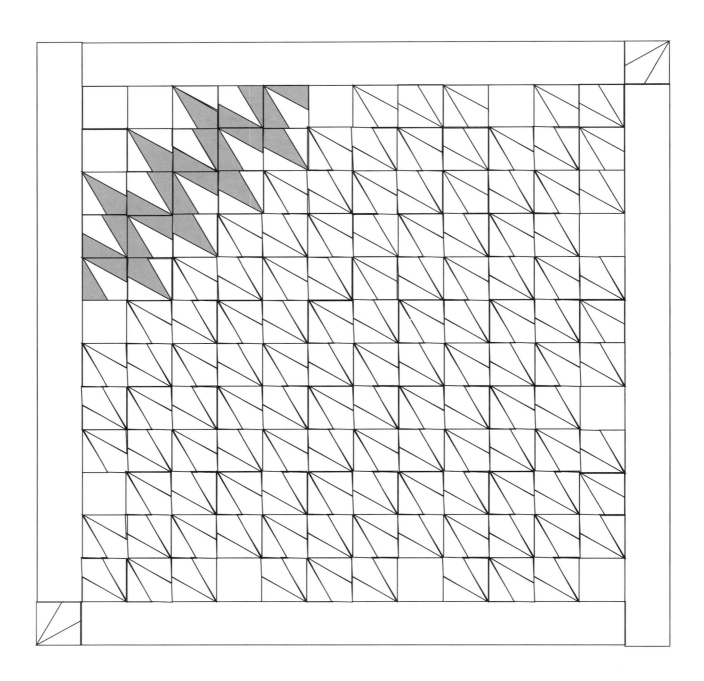

What an exciting tessellation in the colorwash spirit! The challenge in this piece is keeping track of the many combinations of Thirtysomething units.

Color photo: page 28

A patchwork pattern . . . not a dhress size

Quilt size: 42" x 42"

Materials: light through dark of 1 color, 8 values – ½ yd each black – 1½ yds.

NOTE: Arrange fabrics in a pleasing order, making sure there is some degree of contrast from one color to the next. If necessary, renumber the fabrics to correspond with the placement diagram. Fabrics are placed in the following sequence. 1, 5, 1, 6, 2, 7, 3, 8, 4, 5. Paste a swatch of each of the different fabrics in order on a reference card to help you stay organized. Work on small batches and check off the list as they are completed.

Cutting

Read using the patterns on page 15 before beginning to cut.

FABRIC	STRIP WIDTH	NO. OF STRIPS	SUBCUTTING
1 lightest	3⅜"	1	6 rectangles*
	4¼"	1	10 rectangles**
2	5¾"	1	9 rectangles*
	4¼"	1	18 rectangles**
3	5¾"	1	8 rectangles*
	4¼"	1	16 rectangles**
4	5¾"	1	4 rectangles* and 8 rectangles**
5	3⅜"	1	6 rectangles*
	4¼"	1	16 rectangles**
6	5¾"	1	8 rectangles*
	4¼"	1	18 rectangles**
7	5¾"	1	12 rectangles*
	4¼"	2	24 rectangles**
8 darkest	5¾"	1	7 rectangles*
	4¼"	1	16 rectangles**
black	5¾"	1	11 rectangles*
	4¼"	1	14 rectangles**
	3½"	1	12 squares
	3½"	4	borders
	2½"	5	binding

*Cut rectangles 5¾" x 3⅜". Cut diagonally for C triangles.

**Cut rectangles wrong sides together, 4¼" x 2½". Cut diagonally for A and B triangles.

Piecing

1. Piece the following combinations of Thirtysomething units in the quantities indicated, following directions on page 7. Trim units to 3½" square. There will be a few extra triangles.

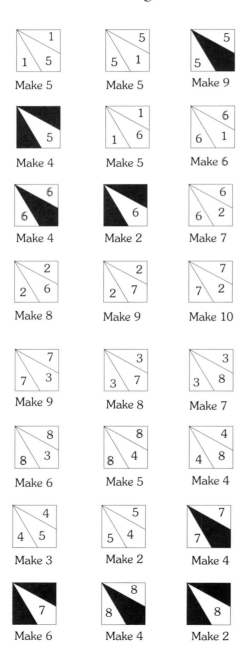

2. Working diagonally, arrange the Thirtysomething units in the order shown in the diagram on the next page. Alternate the direction the Thirtysomething units are pointing and fill in the edges with plain black squares as needed. Sew the units into rows, pressing seams away from the points. Sew the rows together. (See illustration, next page.)

Points to remember: *The seams in the units do not meet when units are pointing in opposite directions.*

3. Add borders to top and bottom, referring to directions on page 15 for measuring the correct length. Sew the remaining 2 units to opposite ends of side borders and sew the borders to the quilt.

A patchwork pattern . . . not a dress size

Rippling Water

■	dark violet
▨	pink
□	light gray
▨	light blue
▨	medium light blue
▨	medium blue
▨	medium dark blue

Quilt size: 48" x 48"
Materials:
  dark violet – 1¼ yds.
  pink – ¼ yd.
  light gray – 1¼ yds.
  light blue – ¼ yd.
  medium light blue – ¼ yd.
  medium blue – ¼ yd.
  medium dark blue– ¾ yd.
  binding – ⅜ yd.
  backing – 3 yds.

This star would make a great medallion for a bed sized quilt. A border of the Opposites Attract block surrounding a "Rippling Water" medallion would make a great splash! **Color photo: page 28**

*Cut rectangles 5¾" x 3⅜". Cut diagonally for C triangles. ▧
**Cut rectangles wrong sides together, 4¼" x 2½". Cut diagonally for A and B triangles.
***Open strips and layer right sides up. Using the line marked 45° on your quilters ruler, cut a 45° angle off the corner of the light gray 3½" strips. Measure along the long edge 22¼" and again cut back at a 45° angle.

Cutting

Read using the patterns on page 15 before beginning to cut.

FABRIC	STRIP WIDTH	NO. OF STRIPS	SUBCUTTING
dark violet	15⅞"	1	2▧ for 4 ◹, and 1⊠ 7¼" x 7¼" for 4 △
	5½"	1	5⊠ for 20 △
	3⅜"	1	4 rectangles*
	4¼"	2	28 rectangles**
pink	5¾"	1	10 rectangles*
light gray	5¾"	2	14 rectangles*
	4¼"	2	24 rectangles**
	3½"	4	8 trapezoids***
light blue	5¾"	1	8 rectangles*
med. lt. blue	4¼"	1	16 rectangles**
med. blue	4¼"	1	16 rectangles**
med. dk. blue	3⅜"	1	6 rectangles*
	3½"	4	border
binding	2½"	5	

A patchwork pattern . . . not a dress size

Piecing

1. Piece the following combinations of Thirtysomething units in the quantities indicated. See directions on page 7. Trim to 3½" square.

Make 12 Make 8 Make 12 Make 16

Make 12 Make 16 Make 4 Make 4

2. Piecing a quarter of the quilt at a time, arrange the Thirtysomething units in the order shown in the diagram. Sew the units into rows, adding violet quarter-square triangles at the end of all but the first row. Press seam allowances away from the points in the rows. Sew the rows together.

3. Sew the 4 sections together. Sew the long edge of the large half-square triangles to the pieced section. Press seam allowance toward the large triangles.

4. Sew a violet quarter-square triangle between 2 light gray border sections. Sew the light gray borders to the quilt, matching centers. Avoid sewing into the seam allowance at the ends of the borders. Match adjacent ends of light gray borders and sew the miter. Backstitch at each end of the seam, but do not sew into the seam allowance.

5. Add the final borders with mitered corners, if desired.

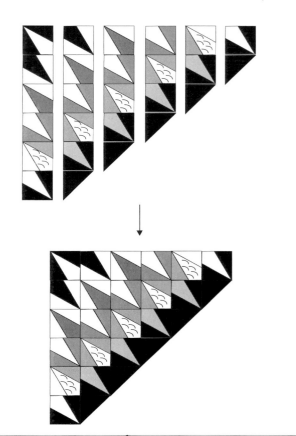

A patchwork pattern . . . or a pieced unit

Wish on a Rainbow

Block size: 12"
Quilt size: 54" x 54"
Materials:
¼ yd. each of the 12
rainbow colors: yellow, violet,
yellow-orange, blue-violet,
orange, blue, red-orange,
blue-green, red, green,
red-violet, yellow-green
black – 3 yds.
backing – 3¼ yds.

It is rare that I use solid colored fabrics, but a pack of hand-dyed fabric in rainbow colors were so luscious, I couldn't resist. The result is this rainbow quilt, made to remind my daughter that I wish her the best always.

Color photo: page 29

*Cut rectangles 4¼" x 2½", wrong sides together. Cut diagonally for 16 A's and 16B's. ◻

**Cut rectangles 5¾" x 3⅜". Cut diagonally for 128 C triangles. ◻

Cutting

Read using the patterns on page 15 before beginning to cut.

FABRIC	STRIP WIDTH	NO. OF STRIPS	SUBCUTTING
black	3⅞"	8	64 ◻ for 128 △
	5¾"	6	64 rectangles**
	3½"	6	border
	2½"	6	binding
yellow, red-orange, blue-green, and violet	3⅞"	2 each	16 ◻ for 32 △ each
yellow-orange, orange, red, red-violet, violet-blue, blue, green, and yellow-green	4¼"	1 each	16 rectangles*

Piecing

1. Piece Thirtysomething units as directed on page 7. Trim to 3½" square.

Make 16 of each color combination and

make 16 each in reverse.

2. Place half-square triangles right sides together and sew on the long bias edge, making 32 half-square triangle units of each color combination.

3. Piece 8 A blocks and 8 B (reverse) blocks. First join the units into rows, then sew the rows together. (See right.)

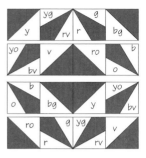

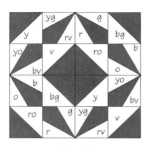

Block A

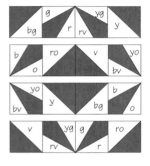

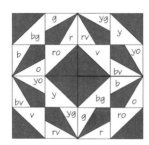

Block B

4. Arrange the blocks in the order shown in the block placement diagram below, rotating the blocks where necessary. Sew the blocks into rows, sew the rows together.

A	B	A	B
B	A	B	A
A	B	A	B
B	A	B	A

5. Add borders, referring to directions on page 15 for measuring the correct length.

Sweet Pepper

Block size: 6"
Quilt size: 51" x 72"
Materials:
  light – 2¾ yds.
  med. and dark scraps = 2½ yds.
  border – ½ yd.
  binding – ⅝ yd.
  backing – 3⅛ yds.

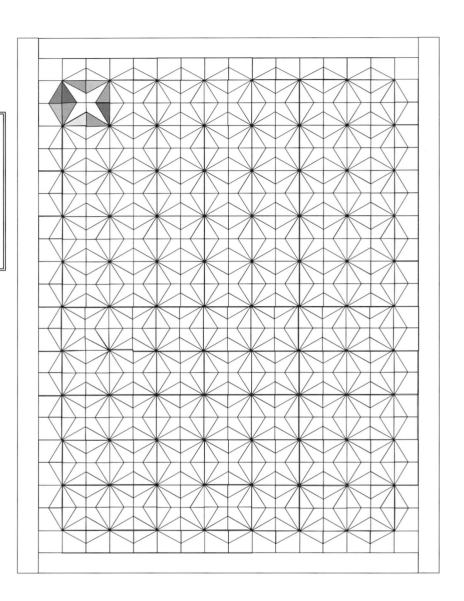

The bright colors are from my large collection of lively little scraps. If all the A triangles are cut from one assortment of scraps and all the B triangles from a different assortment, the same fabrics will not touch when the blocks are sewn together. Equally pleasing is alternating light and dark stars in the warm country tones of gold, red and brown.

Color photo: page 29

*Layer fabric right side up and cut rectangles 4¼" x 2½". Cut diagonally for 314 A triangles. ▱

**Layer fabric right side up and cut light rectangles 4¼" x 2½". Cut diagonally for 314 B triangles. ◹

***Cut light rectangles 5¾" x 3⅜". Cut diagonally for 280 C triangles. ◺

Cutting

Read using the patterns on page 15 before beginning to cut.

FABRIC	STRIP WIDTH	NO. OF STRIPS	SUBCUTTING
scraps	2½"	18	157 rectangles*
	2½"	18	157 rectangles**
light	5¾"	12	140 rectangles***
	3½"	7	72 squares, 3½" x 3½"
border	2"	6	
binding	2½"	7	

A patchwork pattern . . . and a fun technique

Piecing

1. Piece 280 Thirtysomething units as directed on page 7. Trim units to 3½" square. Join 4 units into star blocks.

Make 280.   Make 70.

2. Arrange the blocks to distribute the colors in a pleasing order. Sew the blocks into rows, set 7 across x 10 down. Sew the rows together.

3. Set aside 4 light squares for corners of pieced border. With pairs of squares wrong sides together, trim the corner from 68 squares to make onlies as directed on page 9. Press the seam allowance of A triangles toward the D patch, and press the seam allowance of the E patch toward the B triangle. Sew into 34 pairs.

  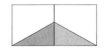

Make 34 of each.

4. Sew pairs end to end to piece 4 border strips. Sew 2 borders containing 20 onlies and 2 borders containing 14 onlies. Sew long border strips to the long sides of the quilt. Sew light squares to opposite ends of the 2 remaining border strips. Sew to the top and bottom of the quilt.

5. Add plain borders, referring to directions on page 15 for measuring the correct length.

Size Option

To make this design queen sized, convert to 4" units. From 5 yds. light, cut 320 C triangles and 76 squares 4½" x 4½" for 72 onlies. Piece 80 stars and set 8 across x 10 down. From medium and dark scraps, cut 338 A triangles and 338 B triangles for the stars and pieced border. Finish with a 6" border for a quilt 84" x 100".

Second Cousins

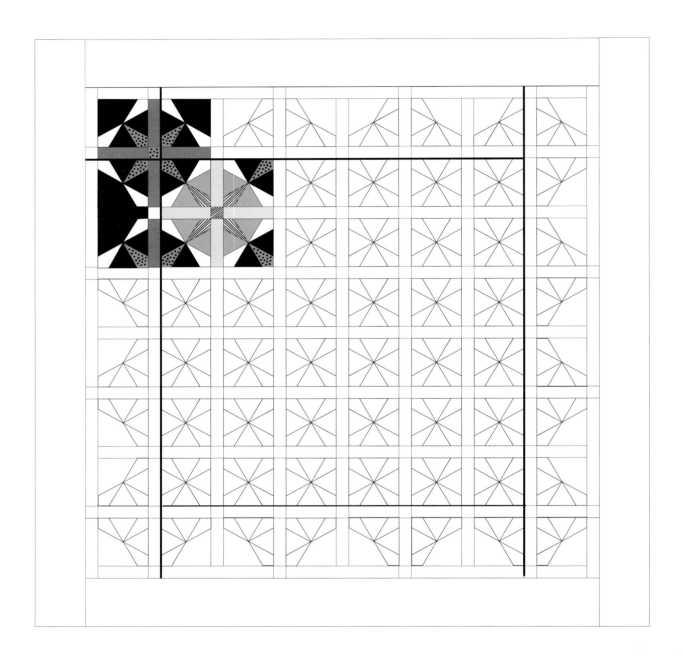

It appears blocks are set on point with a star sashing when more color is introduced to the Fancy X block and set with 2 colors of sashing. Carefully choose the colors for this quilt to get the desired effect. Piecing sample blocks to audition your fabrics is an excellent idea.

Color photo: page 31

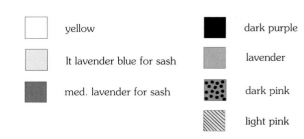

yellow	dark purple
lt lavender blue for sash	lavender
med. lavender for sash	dark pink
	light pink

A patchwork pattern . . . that's easily made

Cutting

Read using the patterns on page 15 before beginning to cut.

FABRIC	STRIP WIDTH	NO. OF STRIPS	SUBCUTTING
dark pink	5¾"	3	32 rectangles*
	2"	1	16 squares, 2" x 2"
light pink	5¾"	2	18 rectangles*
	2"	1	9 squares, 2" x 2"
yellow	5¾"	6	64 rectangles*
	2"	2	40 squares, 2" x 2"
med. lavender	4"	5	72 equilateral triangles
dark purple	4"	8	128 equilateral triangles
	5⅝"	3	28 edge pieces**
	2"	2	12 rectangles 6½" long
	5½"	7	border
	2½"	7	binding
lt. lavender blue	2"	6	36 rectangles 6½" long
dark lavender	2"	19	12 rectangles 14" long & 68 rectangles 6½" long & 4 rectangles 8" long

---

Block size: 6"

Quilt size: 72" x 72"

Materials:
- dark pink – ¾ yd.
- light pink – ½ yd.
- yellow – 1¼ yds.
- medium lavender – 1 yd.
- dark purple – 3 yds.
- lt. lvndr. blue for sash – ½ yd.
- dark lavender for sash – 1¼ yd.
- backing – 4¼ yds.

---

*Open strips and layer fabric right side up. Cut rectangles 5¾" x 3⅜". Cut diagonally for C triangles. Trim tips as directed on page 11.

**Cut 14 dark purple rectangles 5⅝" x 8". Measure over 5⅝" on bottom edge of rectangle and cut back at a 60° angle. Rotate each piece and trim the adjacent side to a 60° angle as shown. After sewing the straight of grain edges will be trimmed when the block is squared to 6½".

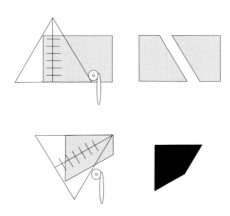

Piecing

1. Piece 36 Fancy X blocks as directed on page 11. Trim to 6½".

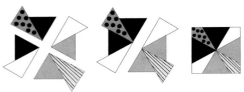

Block A
Make 36.

2. Working in rows, join 4 blocks, a light pink 2" square, and 4 light lavender blue sashing strips into a larger block.

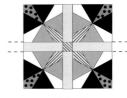

Make 9.

3. Sew a yellow 2" square between 2 dark lavender sashing strips.

Make 24.

4. Referring to the diagram above right, form the center of the quilt by joining the 9 large blocks with 12 dark lavender sashing units and dark pink corner squares setting them 3 across x 3 down. Twelve sashing units remain for step 6.

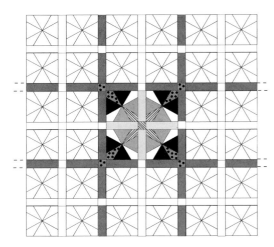

5. Piece 28 edge blocks following block piecing diagram. Trim to 6½".

Block B
Make 28.

6. Assemble the remaining dark lavender sashing pieces, the yellow and dark pink 2" squares and the edge blocks in the rows shown, rotating the edge blocks where necessary. Sew the rows together. Press all seam allowances toward the sashing.

Make 2.

Make 2.

7. Sew the short rows to opposite sides of the quilt. Sew the long rows to the remaining 2 sides.

8. Add dark purple borders, referring to directions on page 15 for measuring the correct length.

Opposites Attract

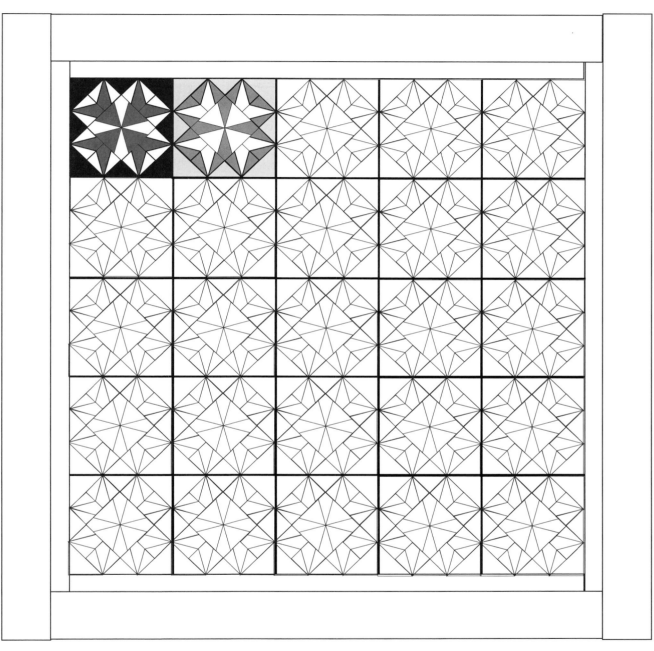

Alternating positive/negative colored blocks is a little used "setting" for quilt blocks, yet the block begged me for this set and the calico print. If you like the block, but getting the points to meet at the edges of the blocks is too challenging, try the alternate setting shown in the quilt plan, "Red Punch".

Color photo: page 30

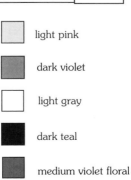

light pink

dark violet

light gray

dark teal

medium violet floral

A patchwork pattern . . . and a fun technique

<table>
<tr><td colspan="2">

Block size: 12¾"
Quilt size: 81" x 81"
Materials:
  light pink – 1⅛ yds.
  dark violet – 1¼ yds.
  light gray – 2⅝ yds.
  dark teal – 2¾ yds.
  med. violet floral – 2 yds.
  binding – ¾ yd.
  backing – 4¾ yds.

</td></tr>
</table>

Cutting

Read using the patterns on page 15 before beginning to cut.

FABRIC	STRIP WIDTH	NO. OF STRIPS	SUBCUTTING
A blocks			
light pink	5½"	2	12 ⊠ for 48 △
	5⅛"	3	24 ◺ for 48 ◹
dark violet	5¾"	2	24 rectangles*
	4¼"	3	48 rectangles**
	4¼"	3	48 rectangles***
light gray	5¾"	4	48 rectangles*
	4"	3	48 equilateral triangles
B blocks			
dark teal	5½"	2	13 ⊠ for 52 △
	5⅛"	4	26 ◺ 52 ◹
	6½"	8	outer border
light gray	5¾"	3	26 rectangles*
	4¼"	4	52 rectangles**
	4¼"	4	52 rectangles***
violet floral	5¾"	5	52 rectangles*
	4"	3	52 equilateral triangles
	3"	8	inner border
binding	2½"	8	

*Open strips and layer all right side up. Cut rectangles 5¾" x 3⅜". Cut diagonally for C triangles. Trim the tip off 48 dark violet and 52 light gray triangles as directed on page 11. ◹

**Layer fabric right side up and cut rectangles 4¼" x 2½". Cut diagonally for A triangles. ◿

***Layer fabric right side up and cut rectangles 4¼" x 2½". Cut diagonally for B triangles. ◺

Piecing

1. Piece Thirtysomething units as directed on page 7. Trim to 3½" square. Sew into pairs.

Make 96
for Block A.

Make 104
for Block B.

2. Piece Fancy X blocks as described on page 11. Trim to 6½" square.

Make 12
for Block A.

Make 13
for Block B.

3. Piece blocks in diagonal rows as shown using quarter-square triangles and half-square triangles for edges and corners of blocks.

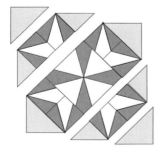 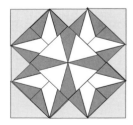

Make 12 Block A.

 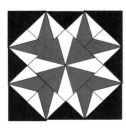

Make 13 Block B.

4. Sew blocks into rows alternating A blocks and B blocks as shown. Sew rows together.

5. Add borders, referring to directions on page 15 for measuring the correct length.

Design Variation – Red Punch

Color photo: page 36

Only the 12 A blocks from the quilt "Opposites Attract" are used in this design for experienced quilters. Cut and piece the A blocks following directions above, making the following substitutions:

> tan for light pink
> dark red for dark violet
> cream for light gray

Set blocks 3 across x 4 down. Use 17 sashing strips cut 2½" x 13¼" between blocks and brown corner squares from scraps cut 2½" x 2½". Add an inner border/sash, and use 7 strips 6" wide for the final border. Red Punch requires:

Block size: 12¾"
Quilt size: 58" x 73"
Materials:
  tan – 1⅛ yds.
  dark red – 1¼ yds.
  cream – 1¼ yds.
  brown sashing and binding – 1½ yds.
  border – 1⅜ yds.
  backing – 3½ yds.

Toe Shoes and Tutus

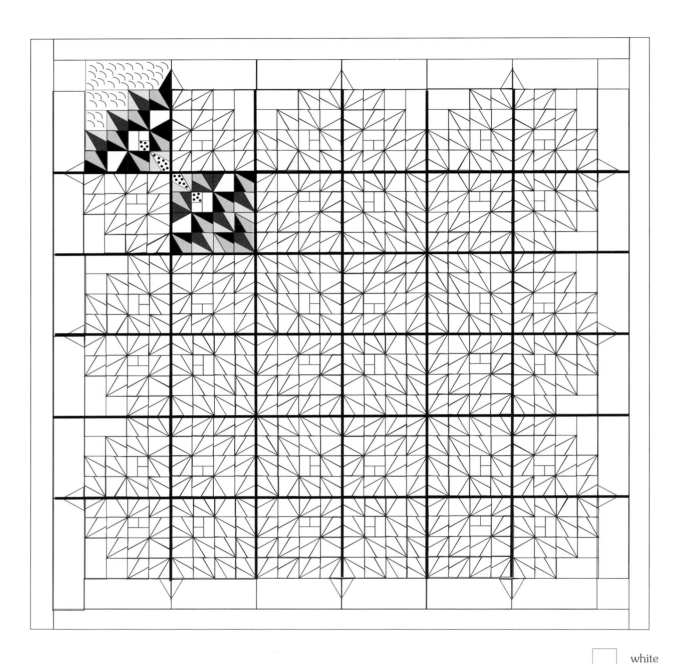

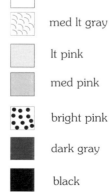

- white
- med lt gray
- lt pink
- med pink
- bright pink
- dark gray
- black

*Layer fabric right side up and cut rectangles $4\frac{1}{4}$" x $2\frac{1}{2}$". Cut diagonally for A triangles.

**Layer fabric right side up and cut rectangles $4\frac{1}{4}$" x $2\frac{1}{2}$". Cut diagonally for B triangles.

***Cut rectangles $5\frac{3}{4}$" x $3\frac{3}{8}$". Cut diagonally for C triangles.

This quilt is not as confusing as you might think. Piecing it as a two-block quilt makes it more manageable, and you will be able to enjoy it all the sooner.

Color photo: page 56

Block size: 12"

Quilt size: 88" x 88"

Materials:
   white – 1¼ yds.
   medium light gray – 2 yds.
   light pink – 1⅜ yds.
   medium pink – 2¼ yds.
   bright pink – ½ yd.
   dark gray – 2⅝ yds.
   black – 2½ yds.
   binding – ¾ yd.
   backing – 8¾ yds.

Cutting

Read using the patterns on page 15 before beginning to cut.

FABRIC	STRIP WIDTH	NO. OF STRIPS	SUBCUTTING
Block A			
light pink	4¼"	5	40 rectangles* and 40 rectangles**
med. light pink	5¾"	5	60 rectangles***
bright pink	5¾"	1	10 rectangles***
	2"	1	
white	3½"	5	40 squares 3½" and
	2"	1	20 rectangles 2" wide
med. light gray	3½"	5	20 squares 3½" and 20 rectangles 6½" wide
dark gray	5¾"	3	30 rectangles***
black	4¼"	5	70 rectangles*
	4¼"	5	70 rectangles**
Block B			
light pink	4¼"	5	40 rectangles* and 40 rectangles**
med. lt. pink	4¼"	1	8 rectangles* and 8 rectangles**
	5¾"	6	64 rectangles***
bright pink	5¾"	1	8 rectangles***
	2"	1	
white	3½"	4	32 squares 3½" and 16 rectangles 2" wide
	2"	1	
dark gray	5¾"	2	32 rectangles***
black	4¼"	8	64 rectangles* and 64 rectangles**
Borders			
black	4¼"	2	6 rectangles* and 6 rectangles**
med. light gray	5"	8	24 rectangles 12½" long & 4 squares 5"
dark gray	6½"	10	borders
binding	2½"	10	

Toe Shoes and Tutus (Cont.)

Piecing

1. Piece the following combinations of Thirtysomething units in the quantities indicated. See directions on page 7. Trim to 3½" square.

Block A - 20   Block A- 120   Block A - 60
Block B - 16   Block B - 96   Block B - 48

Block B - 16   Block B - 16   Block B - 16

2. With pairs of white squares wrong sides together, trim the corner to make onlies as directed on page 9. Press seam allowance of A triangles toward the D patch, and press the seam allowance of the E patch toward the B triangle. Trim to 3½" square.

Make 20 of each for Block A.
Make 16 of each for Block B.

3. Sew together a white 2" strip and bright pink 2" strip. Press seam allowance toward the bright pink. Subcut into 36 units 2" wide.

4. Sew a white rectangle to units made in step 3. Press seam allowance toward rectangles.

Make 20 for Block A.
Make 16 for Block B.

5. Piece the blocks following the block piecing diagrams. Sew the units into rows, then sew the rows together.

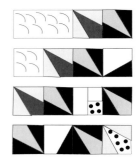 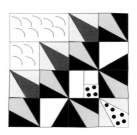

Make 20 Block A.

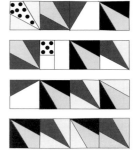 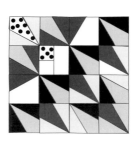

Make 16 Block B.

6. Arrange the blocks in the order shown in the quilt plan, rotating the blocks where necessary. Sew the blocks together into rows, then sew the rows together.

7. With pairs of medium light gray border rectangles wrong sides together, trim a $3\frac{1}{8}$" tall half triangle from the corner. (As directed for onlies on page 9.) Sew on a black A or B triangle. Press seam allowance of A triangles toward the border rectangle, and press the seam allowance of the border rectangle toward the B triangle.

Make 12 and 12 in reverse.

8. Sew 3 pairs of inner border units together, making 4 border strips. Sew 1 of these to opposite sides of the quilt top. Sew the 4 medium light gray squares to opposite ends of the remaining 2 inner border strips. Sew them to the quilt top.

Make 4.

9. Add plain borders, referring to directions on page 15 for the correct length.

Design Variation – Oak Embers

Color photo: page 36

Adding a simple pieced border to 4A blocks makes this quick wallhanging.

Cut 8 light background border pieces $3\frac{1}{2}$" x $12\frac{1}{2}$". Add an only to one end of each to float the star and finish the points. Make the simple pieced border with onlies and reverse onlies. Oak Embers requires:

Unit size: 3"
Quilt size: 36" x 36"
Materials:
   light peach – $\frac{1}{3}$ yd.
   medium peach – 1 yd.
   light background – $\frac{3}{4}$ yd.
   brown print – $\frac{1}{3}$ yd.
   dark brown – $\frac{5}{8}$ yds.
   backing – 1 yd.

Resources

To order the 30 Something Square Up Tool:

    Gaylee Quilting
    N 6628 Bowers Road
    Elkhorn, WI 53121
    (414) 723-7873

To order the Clearview Triangle Tool:

    Clearview Triangle
    8311 180th Street, S.E.
    Snohomish, WA 98296-4802
    (360) 668-4151